WORKPLACE SKILLS: STUDENT BOOK

Textbook and On the Job Training Manual

*From DTR Inc.'s Work Readiness Certification Series
for the second edition of Workplace Skills*

JAY GOLDBERG

Table of Contents

Required Workplace Skills

If someone says he or she is a singer, you expect that person to have a good voice. If someone says he or she is car mechanic you expect them to know how to change a tire and put oil in a car. If someone says he is a running back in the National Football league, you expect him to be a good athlete. I could go on and on, but I'll spare you.

Just like the examples mentioned above, if you say you are a good employee, there are certain skills that supervisors will expect you to possess. Some key ones follow.

Managing your time wisely

Self-management is the ability to understand how to best utilize your time, and the time of other people you interact with on the job, to maximize the work completed by all. Also, to do this without having your supervisor direct you every step of the way.

The areas that are under your control where you need to manage your time wisely include:

- ✓ Getting to work
- ✓ Lunch and breaks
- ✓ Completing work assignments

- ✓ Learning new work tasks
- ✓ Interactions with co-workers
- ✓ Interactions with supervisors
- ✓ Interactions with customers
- ✓ Using company phones for personal use
- ✓ Using the company's (or your personal) email
- ✓ Using the Internet
- ✓ Cell phone use

In all the areas listed, management will expect you manage your time and respect the time of others. If management has to tell you not to spend time talking on your cell phone, just having to tell you is a mark against you. You may think you get a pass because you hadn't been told yet, however, your supervisor will think that was something you should have known without having had to be told.

So do not have your cell phone constantly ringing during work, and do not spend work time making and taking personal calls. To accomplish this you may have to manage your friends and family. For example, let's say you decide to let all your calls go directly to voice mail and to listen to the messages and return any calls you need to during your scheduled break or lunch. That's an excellent personal policy. However, what if the call is for an emergency? You can instruct your family and closest friends to call you two times in a row if there is an emergency and he/she needs to talk to you immediately. Then when you get two calls in row from that family member or friend, take or return the second call immediately (or as soon as possible if you cannot get away at that exact moment). If you call back or take that call because of a real emergency, everyone should understand.

From the Workplace Basics section you know that companies are in business to make profits and the more profits a company makes, the more secure your job is, and the more money the company has available to pay for employee salaries and benefits. An efficient and productive workplace is a key for a business to be able to make profits. Therefore, you need to be a positive factor in the operation of the workplace, not someone who is the cause for work delays, wasted time, and conflict.

For example, you may be on a scheduled work break and decide to stop by and say hello to a friend who works in another area of the company. By doing so, you are preventing that person from completing his/her work. When you do this, no matter what happens, you lose in the eyes of your supervisor. Even if your friend completes all his/her work, your supervisor will believe it was despite your visit. So even if there is no negative impact on the amount of work that is produced; you will be viewed negatively because management will wonder how often you have done this before when there were work delays.

This doesn't mean if you pass a friend's desk and his/her nose isn't buried in work you can't say a quick hello and move on. However, if you want to enter into a discussion, see if you can schedule breaks or lunch together. If possible, your supervisors will comply. If it will cause work problems, your supervisors may not make a change in schedules. Just remember, your supervisors want happy, productive workers, so if it cannot be arranged it will be for a good reason. And you are not owed an explanation.

Another common area where many employees get into trouble is abusing the company's email account or the Internet. Save your personal use of the Internet for home.

Know two things. First, management may read any email in any company email account, even if the email was written to someone outside the company. And assume they will. So never write anything using your company email account that you wouldn't want management to read. That also means the company will know how often and to whom you email using the company email account. So if you make poor self-management decisions and abuse the time you spend writing non-work-related emails using your company email account, management will know it.

Second, every web site you go to on your computer at work, including personal email accounts sites, will be known by your management. Even if you delete the history and the cookies (which is often not allowed to be done by employees, or is allowed as a way to flag Internet abusers), your supervisors will know what web sites you have visited at work. So certainly, do not go to any site you would be embarrassed for your fellow co-workers and management to know you visited. Furthermore, ask what the policy is for using the Internet to go to web sites and to send personal emails when you are on a scheduled break or lunch. Then, of course, follow the company policies.

EXERCISE WS1

Which of the following items are good time management decisions, which are poor time management decisions? Write good or poor for each item below.

Q1. Stopping bye an attractive single person's desk get to know him or her every time you go to get coffee; even though you have to go out of your way to get to that person's desk.

Q2. Stopping bye an attractive single person's desk to get to know him or her every time you go to get coffee since that person's desk is right next to the coffee maker.

Q3. Going to lunch with your co-worker friends so that you can visit with them during lunch rather than visiting with them during work time.

Q4. Discussing a work-related topic with a co-worker as a line of customers backs up at your work station.

Q5. Learning new work tasks during your down time on the job.

*****

Completing tasks accurately and efficiently

At home you may start projects and not complete them. You may have a bookcase with three legs that you started building in 2010, a masterpiece painting that you're waiting to frame, or a half-finished sweater that will no longer fit your best friend's kid anyway. And this may be just fine with you. You enjoyed the ride and the finished product was just a bonus. At work, however, this is not fine.

Completing job assignments in a timely manner is very important. If your supervisor assigns you work and you get it 95% complete, the reaction will not be, "Great job, you almost got the work done." In fact, you will get little credit, if any, for what you completed, even if you did great work.

At work, assignments are not to make you feel good, or to enjoy the ride. If the work is not completed entirely, it serves no purpose and management will look at it as wasted time.

This not only goes for regular work assignments, but for work you do above and beyond your regular assignments. Let's say you see a situation where an Excel spreadsheet will save a lot of time and be more accurate than a manual process that is

9

currently being used on the job. It is not your regular work to create Excel spreadsheets, but you mention to your supervisor how an Excel spreadsheet will benefit the workplace. Your supervisor is thrilled, both because he/she likes the idea and because you are thinking about improvements in the workplace. So your supervisor gives you time to work on the spreadsheet. What just happened is that creating the spreadsheet has now become part of your regular work. There will be expectations that you will complete it. Some of you may be thinking, "I should not have opened my mouth." You would be wrong. Coming up with this idea is the type of workplace behavior that gets you noticed, brings you more in raises, and leads to more responsibility which can eventually lead to a promotion. However, after coming up with the idea, only volunteer, or take on the assignment if you can complete the work. If you do not complete the work, all of the good will (positive reactions) you received for the idea will turn negative. Your supervisor may feel you cannot back up what you say you can do, and may be reluctant to let you implement any more of your ideas.

So complete all work assignments, whether part of your regular work, or extra assignments. If you complete all your assignments in a timely manner, and provide quality work, you will become very valuable to your employer.

EXERCISE WS2

Your supervisor, Arnold D. Terminator, tells you that your job performance has not been up to his expectations. As a supervisor, he is known to fairly represent his name. He has terminated five employees in the last six months. Mr. Terminator informs you that he always has to check your work because you often do not complete tasks assigned to you. This is the same complaint that Mr. Terminator had with the previous five employees who were, gulp, terminated.

You look at your assigned work for the week and know you will have to complete tasks. This week you are assigned to work on and oversee the resolution to the problem dealing with the Freeze Machine, while keeping Mr. Terminator informed of the status through day-end status reports. The Freeze Machine is currently not working. When the Freeze Machine is down, production stops, and that costs the company money both in terms of paying employees who can't work because of the stoppage, and in terms of less product to sell reducing company profits. You know you can find out where in the process it breaks down, even the part of the machine that is not operating properly, and get a history of how often that machine has broken down in the past and been repaired. However, you do not repair machines, and do not have the authority to replace machines.

Q1. What is the specific task that needs to be completed?
Q2. Why is this task needed to be completed?
Q3. Assuming replacing or repairing the Freeze Machine can't happen until tomorrow, what is your last step to take today in your task? Please provide details for that task.
Q4. Since you do not repair machines, and do not have the authority to replace machines, is your task complete after performing the step you wrote in Q3? Explain your answer.

*****

Role of Quality Assurance in the Workplace

Since completing work assignments is not enough (the assignments must be completed correctly and the work product must be of high quality), companies often employ quality assurance practices in the workplace.

11

Therefore, expect your work to be reviewed, either in full, or in part; either all the time, or at random intervals. The main purpose for quality assurance is to verify that the work product is correct and of high quality. A side benefit of the process is that a supervisor can see where additional training is needed for specific employees. It also helps identify the good, the bad and the average, which is used for performance appraisals and determining merit raises.

So quality assurance functions and audits are a normal part of a workplace. They are not the product of an over-controlling boss and management not trusting its employees, or trying to make its employees' lives difficult.

Quality assurance worksheet

1. You work for a manufacturing company that makes car seats for infants. The company has an employee who checks some of your work. List some of the benefits to the company, the company's customers and to you of having this quality assurance person check some of your work.

A. _____
B. _____
C._____
D. _____
E. _____

2. You are a teller for a bank. The company hires mystery shoppers to act as customers. They come into the bank and transact business with a teller and look around the bank. List some of the benefits to the bank, the bank's customers and to you of having this quality assurance person check some of your work.

12

A. _____

B. _____

C._____

D. _____

E. _____

Following instructions and /directions

Instructions are steps you have to follow to complete something properly (such as the instructions for putting together a computer desk). Directions are the proper steps to follow to do something the desired way (such as evacuation procedures in case of an emergency to ensure everyone gets out of the building safely).

Most of us recognize the need to follow instructions. After all we bought the computer desk because we liked it, so we know we have to follow the instructions to ensure it is put together correctly.

On the other hand, many of us balk at following directions. We want to know why. After all there are other ways that the task at hand can be accomplished. Why do I have to go down the hall to the right and all the way across the building to exit during an evacuation when if I made a left there is an exit door right there? Hey, in an emergency I want to get out as fast as I can.

At work you have to think like you are in the army and follow all instructions and all directions exactly. If you believe you have a better way to build the computer desk (better instructions) or a better way to exit the building in an emergency (better directions), then inform your supervisor of your ideas and live by the decision of management.

In all cases, at the time when you are required to follow the instructions or directions, follow them exactly. The time to discuss your ideas for improvement is not at the time the instructions or directions are being followed, it is after the fact to suggest improvements.

Another good idea is to read all instructions in full before starting to follow them. Writing instructions is a skill and not all instructions are written by individuals with expertise in that skill. Most of us have been exposed to the exercise where we have to follow a set of 25 instructions and step #25 says ignore steps 2 thru 24, only do step #1. It is an annoying exercise but it makes it point. If you read the instructions in full you may find that in certain circumstances not all steps need to be followed. For example if you bought the computer desk, a step in middle might say if you didn't purchase the optional light you do not have to punch out the hole on the top shelf. Punching the hole out may have been step two or three and since you do not have the light you may have preferred it without the hole punched out. However, because you did not read all the instructions first you may have punched the hole out before seeing that it wasn't necessary in your case. Also, you may find something confusing at first because you cannot picture it in your head. However, after reading through the entire instructions it becomes clear and you avoid making errors. Finally, by reading through the entire instructions at work, you can jot down your questions and go to your supervisor one time for an explanation/clarification instead of having to keep running back and forth to ask questions which makes you look inefficient (because you were) and a drain on your supervisor's productivity because of the constant stop and starts (all in all, poor time management). In this case many workers see the negative personal signals coming from their supervisors and stop interrupting them. Instead they start guessing at what needs to be done. This can lead to errors in their work, which is an even worse offense than the constant interruption.

So read the instructions in full before starting, jot down all your questions, interrupt your supervisor once to get your questions answered, and get the work completed correctly. The employee who follows these directions (process) for following instructions will be highly-valued by his/her supervisor.

EXERCISE WS3

Follow the directions below and see what you get.

1. Get a blank 8 ½" by 11" piece of paper.
2. With the paper facing you the long way (horizontally), fold the top half way down to the bottom.
3. With the crease at the top, fold the top right and top left corners down to meet the center.
4. Fold the bottom strips up on each side.
5. To make it hold better, fold over each of the four corners at the end of the long strip.

*****

Using Procedure Manuals

Procedure manuals are books written to help employees perform tasks required of them in their jobs. Not all companies have manuals, and those that do may not have them for every job function.

If there is a procedure manual for your job function, it is a very helpful tool to use to ensure that you are doing your job correctly. However, your goal is to become familiar with the procedure manual as quickly as possible so that it becomes a tool to use to complete tasks that are not everyday tasks and not a book to use all the time. Relying too much on a procedure manual can slow you down. So employers expect new employees to rely on procedure manuals more than experienced employees.

When you are presented with a procedure manual read it completely to get an idea of what will be expected of you on the job and to understand how the procedure manual is laid out so you can easily find specific information in the manual. After you have worked on the task for a few days and are starting to get a good feel for how it is done, reread the procedure manual to start absorbing the job functions in full. By rereading the manual after performing the job function live, you may find that the procedures make more sense to you.

EXERCISE WS4

Indicate whether the situation below is good or poor use of a procedure manual.

Q1. Jim has worked for a Paper company for 8 years. A customer asks for special shipping procedures that Jim has not used in over 5 years.

Q2. Pam has worked for a Paper Company for 8 years as well. A customer calls and asks her to send him the same letter she has sent to him many times before.

Q3. Nellie is a new hire for a Paper Company and is performing a task she just learned two days ago.

*****

Ethics

In Stephen King's epic tale of good versus evil, *The Stand*, all of the survivors of a biological catastrophe are driven to split up into two camps; the good camp (Mother Abigail), and the evil camp (Randall Flagg). There was no middle ground.

It is the same with ethics. A behavior is either ethical (right) or unethical (wrong). There is absolutely no gray area. Being ethical means doing the right thing. What determines whether something is ethical or unethical is the behavior itself, not the circumstances surrounding the action taken, not the relationship between the people involved, not an individual's culture, not a person's value system, not life's experiences, etc., etc., etc.

If you were robbed by someone who needed the money to feed his/her kids, the act of robbery makes this an unethical behavior. In this case, surrounding circumstances such as that the robbery was out of desperation for the robber who needed to have money to feed his/her children is irrelevant when determining whether or not the act was ethical. Stealing is wrong, hence it is unethical. Besides, who's to say that the money he/she stole from you wasn't going to make it difficult for you to feed *your* kids?

That said, people are unethical all the time and being unethical does not make someone a bad person. For example, breaking the law is wrong, hence unethical. How many of you have driven a little over the speed limit? Well, that is against the law, making it an unethical act, but it does not make you a bad person.

The key to understanding ethics is to be able to define whether an act is ethical or unethical. Once you have identified the ethical behavior, then you decide what to do. In other words, to either do the ethical behavior or do the unethical behavior. This is where circumstances, relationships, culture, values, life's experiences, etc., etc., etc. come into play. You decide in each situation if you are going to act ethically or unethically.

There will be times in life that you feel strongly that choosing the unethical behavior is the right choice for you. However, you must be aware that if you choose to do the unethical behavior there can be **severe consequences**. Therefore, if you choose to act unethically, know what those consequences can be, and be prepared to accept those consequences for making the decision to act unethically. In the case of the person who committed the robbery above, let's say that the individual came in, explained his/her situation and you gave them $100 for food out of the store's cash register. You may feel strongly that helping that person's family was the right thing to do. However, you just stole money from your place of employment. A consequence of your action could be that you get fired when the amount in the register doesn't box to the day's activity.

More realistically, let's say that as soon as your boss comes back you tell him/her what you did and that you want him/her to take the $100 out of your next pay check. Now instead of stealing, you forced your employer to loan you $100. That is also wrong, hence unethical. You cannot force someone to loan you money. You could still get fired and be charged with stealing. Your boss could also say okay and take the money out of your next check. In either case what you did was unethical, only in one case there was a consequence (being fired) and in another there were no consequences. The key, however, is that you thought it through, knew the potential consequences, and decided that performing the unethical act was worth the risk to you. In this case it was an unethical act you thought was the right thing to do.

As a side note, this is a case where you acted unethically because of your value system. It's possible; however, that your boss' value system was different. He/she may have called someone they knew who worked for the local Workforce Development Board to arrange a meeting between that person and a Job Counselor to help that person get a job. That would have been teaching that person to fish (long term solution) rather than giving him/her money to buy fish (short term solution). This is a good example why the ethics of a situation comes down to the underlying behavior and ignores items such as personal values.

Next, let's look at the possible consequences for the unethical act of robbery from the parent's (robber's) point of view. The parent who stole from you may have felt he/she had no choice because he/she had to feed his/her kids. When making that choice, he/she should have been prepared for a possible arrest for committing the unethical, illegal act of robbery, and worse, for potentially losing his/her children if Social Services now deemed him/her an unfit parent. In the driving scenario, if you choose to drive over the speed limit, you have to be prepared to pay a speeding ticket, see your insurance rates increase, and know that you may have given the police officer cause to search your vehicle.

19

The case of Don Imus

Imus was the morning Dee Jay on "W*O*L*D", I mean WFAN (sorry, I just like that old Harry Chapin song). His show was simulcast on MSNBC. As a shock jock, saying outrageous things was part of his job. One morning on his show, during an impromptu comedy routine, Imus used derogatory terms (not serious, in jest) in his public forum to describe members of the predominately African-American women's basketball team at Rutgers University. In his professional life, Imus is very charitable, allowing his national radio show to be used for fund raising by charities for causes such as SIDS (Sudden Infant Death Syndrome). In his personal life, he is even more charitable having established the Imus Ranch for kids with cancer, a working cattle ranch surrounded by an old western town. Children with cancer come to the ranch and work the ranch alongside of Imus and his family. Therefore, not only does Imus spend money on kids with cancer, but he spends time with them as an active participant interacting during their visits. Children of all races and creeds attend his ranch.

Was Imus' remark ethical or unethical? When determining the ethics, first eliminate the surrounding circumstances. That means the fact that he is a shock jock and therefore expected to say some outrageous things, is irrelevant when determining the ethics. Don't agree? Well, is it okay for a hitman to kill someone because it's his/her job? Also, the fact that he is very charitable, and that he helps people of all races and creeds are also irrelevant. Using a public forum to denigrate (even in jest) college kids is wrong. Therefore, it is unethical. Does this make Imus a bad person? No, he does a lot of good in his life. It's possible the fact that he was doing his job and that he has a solid record of doing good made him feel that he could say what he did and it would be understood that he meant no harm. Irrelevant! Surely his loyal listeners would know that he said it in jest and he meant no harm. Irrelevant! The reality of the situation is that being on the public airways meant that people who were not his listeners would hear about it and react to it. Even that is irrelevant! It is the underlying behavior (using public airways to denigrate college kids) that determined his action to be unethical. And remember, doing something unethical means that there could be consequences. Were there consequences for Don Imus? Yes, he and his staff were fired, and his reputation took a hit from people who primarily knew of Imus through this event. While Imus made it back on the air on a different radio station, and is simulcast on a television station that does not currently go into as many homes as MSNBC, he still paid a price for his unethical act. It just wasn't a life sentence.

Let's say that there were no consequences to Don Imus; that the comment went through with no reaction. Would that have changed the ethics of the situation? Of course it would not have. The behavior is the same regardless of the consequences paid for the unethical act. Certainly the person who gets away with murder is not ethical, while the person who gets caught for committing murder is unethical. All unethical acts bring the possibility of consequences. Not all unethical acts have consequences attached to them. If you drove ten miles over the speed limit and there were no radar traps, cameras, or police officers around, you won't get a ticket. However, you still performed an illegal, hence an unethical act. By driving ten miles an hour over the speed limit, you were willing to risk getting a ticket and were prepared to pay a fine if you were caught. After all, if you weren't prepared for the possible consequences, you shouldn't have been speeding.

Music downloads

The Internet is amazing technology. It allows people all over the world to access other peoples' computers. That includes the ability to copy files from one computer to another computer. That is called downloading.

So networks were created for individuals to share music files. Someone would buy a music CD, copy the songs on the CD to their computer's hard drive, and allow other people to access their computer and download the songs. That one CD could now be owned by hundreds, if not thousands of people. How nice. How giving. How unethical.

The artists who wrote the songs and recorded the album certainly were not expecting to share the royalties (profits) of one CD amongst thousands of customers. Downloading music for free is directly stealing money from the record company and the band that recorded the CD. Not to mention retailers who would have generated sales to some of the people who would have bought the CD if they could not get it for free and the workers who lost their jobs because the retailers were not making as much money. In addition, music is copyrighted material so downloading it for free is against the law which is another fact in making it unethical. Of course, the ethical way to download music is to pay for the songs you download at websites like iTunes, which is legal and results in royalties for the artists.

Since downloading music without paying is unethical, that means that there are potential consequences for downloading music for free. What are those potential consequences? The obvious is that if caught, you could pay significant fines. Don't believe me? The RIAA (Record Industry Association of America) website posted a write-up on December 6, 2007 indicating that 396 pre-litigation letters (sent out to settle before pursuing a lawsuit) have been sent to individuals (primarily students) at 22 universities.

The settlement figure is thought to be around $750 per song; so illegally downloading only 5 songs would cost someone $3,750 to settle. If these college kids do not settle and go to court, they are risking a lot more in money damages. Jamie Thomas, a single mother of two, was ordered to pay the RIAA (representing the record labels) $222,000 worth of damages for 24 pirated songs. Remember, only the behavior determines the ethics, the fact that Jamie Thomas is a single mother of two is irrelevant when determining the ethics in this situation.

Think the punishment doesn't fit the crime? **First**, when you act unethically it is not you who decides what the consequences will be for that unethical act. It is the damaged party or the court system. **Second**, "according to non-profit research group Institute for Policy Innovation, global theft of sound recordings cost the U.S. economy $12.5 billion in lost revenue and more than 71,000 jobs and $2 billion in wages to U.S. workers per year." This quote is from the RIAA website in a write-up *RIAA Pre- Lawsuit Letters Go To 22 Campuses In New Wave Of Deterrence Program* posted on December 6, 2007.

It seems to me that illegally downloading music is kind of like playing the lottery in reverse. With the lottery you pay $1 to buy a ticket to try to win a lot of money. And only a few random people win. With the illegal downloading of music, instead of paying $1 to buy a song, you download it for free and try to avoid paying a lot of money (if caught). And only a few random people lose.

Let's also look at this issue from the band's perspective. If a band puts out new albums on CDs and does not generate sufficient income from those albums, the band could break up and stop making new music. After all, they need to eat. Some bands are better studio bands than live bands and some

23

musicians like making music but do not like to tour. These bands would quickly disappear if the band could not earn money from the sale of its albums.

On the same front: if you are using portions of this book from photocopies; that may also be a copyright infringement, making it illegal, and unethical. Writing this book is something I have done to not only help the readers, but to put food on my table.

Worksheet: ethics work scenario #1

Let's say you work for a bank as a teller. Stated in the qualifications for the job is that you <u>must</u> have a high school diploma or GED. One day a co-worker mentions to you that he/she is really excited because next month he/she is finally getting his/her GED. Your co-worker is a great worker, in fact last month he/she won employee of the month for the third month in a row. What are the ethics in this situation for both your co-worker and yourself?

_____

_____

_____

_____

_____

_____

_____

_____

_____

_____

_____

_____

_____

_____

My take on ethics scenario #1

For your co-worker the ethics are straight forward. The fact that he/she was untruthful on the job application is in violation of company rules and, therefore, an unethical act. What are the consequences? If found out, that employee could (and most likely would) be fired even though he/she was a top employee.

What about the situation you are in? The ethical behavior would be to inform your supervisor. I know, I know, many of you are thinking that is not what you would do. I'm sure some of you feel that telling your supervisor is snitching and you are no snitch. Others of you feel that it is not your job; that is/was either the Human Resources Department job or your supervisor's job to find this out. So many of you would not inform your supervisor, you would just let the comment go.

What you are doing is applying your own set of values to the situation and deciding that acting unethically is the correct action to take. I am not going to preach about what you should do. Just remember that acting unethically (which does not make you a bad person) comes with potential consequences. Don't think there is any possibility of consequences here? Think again my friend.

Let's say that your supervisor finds out that your co-worker did not have his/her high school diploma or GED when he/she was hired. Maybe your co-worker celebrates when he/she finally gets the GED, or someone sends that person flowers as congratulations. When your co-worker is called onto the carpet by his/her supervisor, your co-worker comments that he/she didn't think it was a big deal and that he/she mentioned it to you and you did not think it was a big deal either. That statement by your co-worker just brought you into this mess.

As a result of the lie on the application your co-worker gets fired (this is usually a policy; companies cannot start looking into the degree of each lie on a job application). Nothing happens to you. You keep your job and, in fact, have no idea that your name was brought up in the meeting between your now fired ex-co-worker and your supervisor. However, your supervisor now feels that your priorities are wrong. You do not have the best interests of the company in mind. If you thought you would be admired for not "tattling" on a co-worker who was untruthful on his/her job application, you may be by some misguided co-workers, but you won't be by people of influence in the company.

A year later there is a promotion opportunity in the company. You believe you are perfect for the job. You don't get it. The same thing happens nine months later, then fifteen months after that. Unfair (you think)! However, it all goes back to your having deciding to act unethically. It is the fact that management in the company does not believe they can count on you to do the right thing for the company that is preventing you from advancing in the company. And you have totally forgotten that event, and never got a chance to explain your side of things, although I doubt that that would have made a difference anyway.

This happens all the time. Everyone is held accountable for how they act in the workplace. And more often than not, workers are unaware of how much management knows about what is going on. You are judged more by your supervisor's observations on what is going on and comments by third parties than you would believe.

Therefore, often consequences for choosing to do an unethical act are hidden consequences. Sometimes you hear people saying," I have had a run of bad luck." Perhaps that bad luck is really just hidden consequences from unethical behaviors (not karma, but direct results like not getting the promotion in this example). Or, maybe it is just bad luck.

Now here's the million (or at least thousand) dollar question. What would your author, Jay Goldberg do in this situation?

First, I would immediately recognize that my co-worker put me in an uncomfortable situation. This is a situation I did not ask to be in, and would not have volunteered to be in. Second, I would understand that people usually act for a reason. What my co-worker was doing was bringing in another person (me) to their situation. He/she may never have to use the "Jay Goldberg card" (e.g. telling the boss Jay knew and didn't think it was a big deal); but it was there if needed. Third, I would know that what my co-worker did was wrong and, therefore, unethical. Fourth, I would understand that my co-worker placed me in a position where I would have to act ethically or unethically. What I would not do, is ignore the situation like it never happened. I would make a decision based on full knowledge of what could happen if I were to choose to say nothing.

Okay, okay, I'll give you my decision based on the ethics and my personal set of values. I would approach my co-worker and tell him/her that he/she placed me in an uncomfortable situation. That he/she knows full well that you have to have your high school diploma or GED to be a bank teller. I would then tell him/her that he/she needs to speak to our supervisor and inform our supervisor of the situation. Furthermore, I would tell my co-worker that if he/she did not do this, that I would have no choice but to tell our supervisor myself. I would finish up by telling my co-worker that I am extremely angry with him/her for having put me in this position.

That is how I would handle the situation. Some of you will not agree with how I handled this. That's okay. I wouldn't risk my career because a co-worker was untruthful on a job application and decided to make me part of the lie.

Now, what if unbeknownst to my co-worker and myself was that the bank policy for mandatory high school diplomas or GEDs for all tellers came about when a major client of this fictional bank had numerous severe errors when conducting business with the bank's tellers seven years ago. The errors were all done by under-qualified tellers. To keep that client, the bank started a policy that all tellers would have at least a high school diploma or GED and promised that major client it would comply with that requirement 100%. Based on that promise the client stayed with the bank and became the #1 account for the bank in terms of profitability. Every year, the client reminds senior bank management of the bank's promise to only hire tellers with high school diplomas or GEDs.

Would this change your thinking, or at least provide you with a better understanding of why you would have shot yourself in the foot if you had acted unethically in this situation?

As an aside, "I'm not a tattler" is a playground stance, not a recognized position in the law. Ever hear of aiding and abetting? Or obstruction of justice? Or perjury? I don't think law officials or judges will say, "That's okay, you knew of a crime, or you know who committed a crime, but I respect you; you're no tattle tail." Consider the Personnel Department the law official and Management the judge for the workplace.

Worksheet: ethics work scenario #2

What if your supervisor asks you to do something that is illegal? For example, your supervisor asks you to not ring up a

sale to avoid reporting the sale for sales tax purposes. What are your thoughts regarding this situation?

_____

_____

_____

_____

_____

_____

_____

_____

_____

_____

_____

_____

_____

_____

_____

_____

My take on ethics scenario #2

Obviously, not reporting all sales to stiff the government of the proper sales tax is illegal, and therefore, unethical, so you should not agree to do this. Even if you agree that taxes are too high (who doesn't); if sales taxes are underreported, the government will just find its money elsewhere. Maybe your real estate taxes will increase because your supervisor (and others like him/her) is not paying what is properly owed.

But your supervisor told you to do it.

What your supervisor tells you does not supersede the law. It is not an excuse to the court that you were only doing what your boss told you to do. Besides, if caught and faced with fines, want to bet how stand up your supervisor would be. I would bet your supervisor would know nothing about you not ringing up the sales, especially if he/she was not ringing up sales to avoid paying sales tax; but to steal money from the company. How quickly do you think it would take for your supervisor to blame you for the thefts? You'd be fired on the spot. And then, what if the owners decided to make you an example of you for his/her other employees, and had you prosecuted.

Even if the truth came out in court, your supervisor was arrested, and you were cleared of any wrongdoing; you would still have legal fees, lots of stress, and be out of a job. Telling the owner that you knew your supervisor was not ringing up all sales, but thought it was for cheating the government out of sales tax and not that he/she was stealing money from the company, would not result in you saving your job.

Unethical behaviors can have serious consequences. Do not act unethically just because your supervisor told you it is "okay" or even "expected." Remember, your personal values, etc. are not part of determining the ethics of any situation. So if you agree with your supervisor's position and perform the unethical act, just know you may have to pay the consequences for that unethical act alongside your supervisor. If you constantly are put in these kind of difficult situations, transfer to another department, talk to Human Resources, or find another employer.

Worksheet: ethics work scenario #3

You work in a donut shop. "Mmm, donuts!" Every morning on their way to work your buddies stop there to say hi and eat. Most days you are there with your supervisor. On rare occasions when your supervisor is not there with you, you give your friends free coffee. You know that this game of your friends guessing when they will get free coffee is the only reason that they come every day. It's the fun, not the money. If you stopped doing this your friends might drop by once a month instead of five times a week. Even when they get the free coffee, they spend a lot of money on breakfast sandwiches, donuts and more. What are your thoughts regarding this situation?

_____

_____

_____

_____

_____

_____

_____

_____

_____

_____

_____

_____

_____

_____

_____

_____

My take on ethics scenario #3

First, let's look at the ethics. Giving customers, even friends and relatives, free merchandise (food in this case) is stealing. What if you worked in a music store instead and you were giving away free CDs, not free coffee. Or if you worked in an electronics store and the merchandise you were giving away were free flat screen, high definition, televisions. The underlying behavior is the same in all of these cases. What the actual product being given away for free is does not matter. That is irrelevant.

In this situation you might know that if you were not giving the

31

occasional free coffee away that it would cost the business money in the long run because your friends would stop coming every day. Furthermore, you might have worked previously for a restaurant that would occasionally buy their loyal repeat customers a drink because it was good for business. And in your observation it was not just good for business, but great for business. In fact, your past experience is the reason you decided to give the free coffee on occasion to your buddies. And it worked out great for the Donut Shop. They now come in every day.

All of that is irrelevant when deciding the ethics of the situation. If the business you work for has a different view about a policy that worked well in your prior business, it is not your place to independently implement your own rules, even if you truly believe it would be for the good of your employer.

Now, you may ask, "so Jay you told me that the profitability of my employer is very important to me, and now you tell me I should *not* do something that is bringing in more profits to the business?" Huh?

In this scenario what I would do is have a talk with my supervisor and explain the old policy at the restaurant where I used to work. I would then inform him/her what I would like to do for my friends because I believed it would result in them coming to the Donut Shop more often and, in the long run, be a more profitable situation for the business.

Then I would be prepared to follow whatever the supervisor stated was the policy of the Donut Shop.

Remember, you do not know the whole story. It's possible that this was tried before and got out of hand with employees giving away too much free stuff. It is also possible that the Donut

Shop had complaints in the past from customers because they saw/heard that some other customers got free coffee while they never did. Maybe, when customers stop coming as often and do not get free coffee, they get angry and never come again. It could also be that you were giving away the product (coffee) that has the largest profit margin, and that the profits from the other food are minimal. In that case, maybe your supervisor tells you not to give free coffee, but is okay to give a free donut. What worked for one business may have been tried and did not work for another business. Also, you are not privy to the profit model for the company that has employed you.

Stealing from an employer is not only stealing money

While the scenario above is an obvious case of stealing a product from an employer, another less obvious theft is stealing your wages.

If you show up late, extend breaks and lunches, leave early, do personal business on your employer's time, etc., you are being paid by your employer for time that you are not working for your employer. Stealing time, therefore, is stealing money, which is unethical and comes with potential consequences.

Likewise, if you show up to work drunk, high, or hung over, you have put yourself in a position to be less productive on the job, which again is stealing money since you are being paid to be at your best. This is also unethical and, if caught, can come with severe consequences.

The Employee Handbook

Ethics in the workplace has an additional item that employees must pay attention to; the Employee Handbook. This can be a formal document, informal memos, or even word of mouth.

As long as the rules of this employer do not violate ethics (underlying behaviors, not your values), then if you do not follow the rules, your behavior is unethical. That means consequences could follow. You could be fired from your job.

So, know the rules of your workplace, and follow them.

EXERCISE WS5

During this work readiness and customer service training program you develop a quick friendship with someone who will be in the program with you. In fact, you make plans with that person to get together over the weekend. That person tells you that he/she has serious financial problems at home. During the first day of this program you learn that there are businesses that will hire graduates right away at a good wage to work part time if they pass all assessments and competencies. Your initial thought is that this is an excellent opportunity for your new friend.

When you get together over the weekend with your new friend he/she tells you that you wouldn't believe the great luck he/she had. When leaving the building he/she saw a Teacher Guide on a desk in an unattended room. He/she then goes on to say that the guide has all then answers to the exercises and quizzes, even some lame exercise about business ethics. He/she further states that since you two are friends, you are the only person with whom he/she will share the answers. He/she also states that this is a great opportunity for him/her to complete the program, and get a job that is critical to his/her family's eating well.

Q1.   Did the person who took the Teacher Guide do an ethical or unethical act?

Q2.   Explain your answer.

Q3.   What is the ethical thing for you to do?

Q4.   If you decided to say nothing, but did not use the answers, what would happen if your friend was caught and said, "It's no big deal. Even <you> knew about it and didn't think it was a big deal", and you were doing very well in the program?

Q5.   If your friend was not caught, what negative consequences could happen because of his/her cheating?

*****

Reading in the Workplace

The goal of education is to teach knowledge and skills, not to get students "ready for work." Toward that end, when teaching reading, the education system unintentionally provides some information that goes against how that skill is best applied in the workplace. Reading in the workplace is different than reading outside the workplace. Reading a novel is different than reading a memo at work.

When you were taught reading in school you were encouraged to "read between the lines." It is not just what is written, but what the author's real meaning is behind the actual words on the page. Debates are held in classrooms all across America about the "real meaning" behind a cleverly written passage in a book. When reading a mystery novel, readers are encouraged to look for clues to help solve the mystery before it's revealed by the author. At times a book is vague because the author wants you to fill in the blanks yourself so you will be surprised when you read what actually happens (or feel good when you guessed the correct outcome).

This is not true when reading memos at work. There is no reading between the lines, there is no "solving mysteries" and if something is vague, you do not fill in the blanks yourself.

A work document is straightforward. It says what it means and there are no hidden meanings. If you are reading something into a document that is not stated directly, then your thinking is probably wrong. If you believe a work document is hinting at something that is not directly stated, ask your supervisor for clarification. Do not assume. This is also how workplace rumors start. Someone "reads between the lines" of a business memo; mentions his/her thoughts to a co-worker, and a rumor starts spreading. Eventually the starting place of the rumor is forgotten, and the topic of the rumor is thought to be have been said directly by someone in the company. So don't read between the lines, take workplace memos at face value, and ask questions for clarification if you are unsure of anything.

Another way that leisure reading and workplace reading differs is that when reading a novel, the author expects readers to bring preconceptions with them. That is not the case when reading memos at work. If I told you that Pat was a gold digger and then asked you to describe Pat, your first thought might be that Pat is someone who is looking to marry for money. However, what if in reality Pat works in a mine, digging for gold.

Again, your preconceptions can nudge you into reading more into a business memo than what is there. For example a memo may contain the following:
"We have become aware that not everyone is wearing a safety helmet when using machine ABC. It is a serious offense not to wear a safety helmet. If we catch anyone in the future without his or her helmet on, we will be forced to let them go."

Now from the Workplace Basics section, you know that this is written from two points of view: management's concern for its employees, and management's concern for violating OSHA rules and regulations.

However, if a co-worker reads this memo and brings to the table the preconceptions that management is snooping on its employees, or that management is too controlling; he/she might interpret the memo in a negative way. That co-worker may tell you:

"Did you read that memo; management is treating us like kids. If I want to risk not wearing a safety helmet who are they to tell me what to do. I bet they are looking for reasons to fire us."

This statement can start rumors. When spread throughout the company, it could end up being shortened to, "Management is looking to fire people." The original source, a misguided employee brining his/her preconceptions to a business memo and "reading between the lines", gets lost in translation.

Reading perceptions group discussion worksheet (write the answers on a board for all three, then go to page 51 to continue the discussion)

In the next story Jack is a professional basketball player. Without reading the story, what do you know about Jack?

_____
_____
_____
_____
_____

In the next story Robin is a cheerleader. Without reading the story, what do you know about Robin?

_____
_____
_____
_____
_____

3. On his first day on the job, Stu was nervous and shook hands with his boss using his left hand. Did Stu do anything wrong?

_____

_____

_____

_____

_____

In all of these examples you will have an image of the person and situation just based on the brief description supplied to you. In fictional writing, the author often counts on that to help cement the character in your mind, or to make the character appear more real to you because you compare that character to someone you know.

That is not the case at work; do not bring preconceptions to business memos. Ask questions, do not assume.

Speed reading

A slow reader will read every word in a sentence, one at a time. If this describes the way that you read, notice how many times your eyes move as you proceed across a line of text. Reading every word and "fixing" your eyes on each word requires a considerable amount of time. Before you get to the end of a long sentence, chances are you have forgotten the beginning of that sentence, so you look back at the beginning - just to make sure that you got all of the information. The same process occurs with paragraphs, or with whole essays or textbook chapters.

If you train yourself to read quickly, rather than slowly, you will notice that several changes will occur in the way that you absorb and remember information from your reading.

✓ You will move your eyes fewer times, so you get through a reading passage more quickly.

✓ Since you get through a reading passage more quickly, you will be more likely to remember what you have read without having to look back to the beginning of a long sentence. This ability to remember more happens when you begin to process ideas, rather than single words.

✓ You will finish reading assignments more quickly and remember what you have read more accurately.

Reading for main topic

The main idea is, most often, stated in a topic sentence of a paragraph. In effective business documents, the topic sentence is usually the first sentence in the paragraph, but it may be the last sentence or any other sentence. The remaining sentences in the paragraph add supporting details to explain or tell more about the main idea. More than one paragraph may give supporting details about one main idea. In the paragraph that follows, the first sentence is the topic sentence. It states the main idea of the paragraph. The other sentences add information to explain the main idea.

Every good music collection needs albums by Al Stewart. Most know Al Stewart from two songs, "Year of the Cat" and "Time Passages." However, he has many other excellent songs, and all of his albums are high quality from first song to last song. In addition, Al Stewart is unique in that he writes rock (or folk rock) songs about events in history. In fact one of his albums, *Between the Wars*, has songs that chronicle events from 1918 to 1939.

The main topic here is "Every good music collection needs albums by Al Stewart."

41

Reading for details

There are two ways to read for details. The first is when you are reading to absorb all the information contained in the piece you are reading. The second is when you are trying to find the answer to a specific question.

Reading for details: absorbing all information

When reading to absorb all information, you need to read the entire document, understand the main topic(s) and focus on the key characteristics for the topic(s). At work, this information will be vital to your job, so you need to take notes to help you remember the key points that you read. Taking notes also allows you to quickly review key points so that you do not have to go back to the original document and find that information again.

Your notes should be in the form of:

Topic   Specific item 1
                                Specific item 2
                                Specific item 3

Using the Al Stewart piece, the notes, containing the details of the write-up would be:

Best known songs   "Year of the Cat"
                                "Time Passages"

Album characteristics   Good songs throughout
                                Songs and entire albums about
                                events in history

After taking notes, you should read and review your notes from time to time to help you remember what you read. Also remember that it has been proven that reading quickly helps with long term memory more than reading slowly.

Additional note taking methods

In addition to writing down notes you can use a yellow highlighter to highlight key points (assuming you own the source material). If you do not own the material make a work copy for yourself (if feasible) and use a highlighter on your work copy. If you do not want to mark up your original copy, use yellow stick'em notes and write the key points on those and stick them to the appropriate page.

Reading to find specific information

When reading to find specific information, you do not need to read the full text. You can skim to find the specific information you require (do not read every word; look for a key word or words; can use finger to help guide you while skimming).

EXERCISE WS6

Skim the flash fiction story below to determine **the name of the famous educated rapper**. Please skim the story, do not read it. The purpose is the find the answer to the question as quickly as you can. If you want to read it in full after the exercise, I will be honored. I wrote this piece for a flash fiction contest at Associated Content. For the contest I had to write a flash fiction piece starting with the line, "He had not been expecting a letter." Associated Content has been absorbed by Yahoo.

You only have three minutes to complete this exercise. Wait until the instructor says start.

Life's Little Annoyances

He had not been expecting a letter. Especially since letters had gone the way of high-def televisions, digital cameras and video cell phones; so last century.

After giving the postmaster private a hundred dollar bill, and getting a dirty look for such a small tip; the man looked at the letter. For a long moment he stood there just staring at the darn thing until he remembered that he was actually going to have to read it himself. He thanked the Alien Who Is Our God that he took the reading elective in college.

The letter was dirty, crumpled and looked very old. In fact the letter was very old. There was an expiration date in red in the upper right corner. That date couldn't be true thought the man, the date was in the 1990's.

Confused and a little scared, the man's mind went racing. His first thought was that the letter was from the "Time of Viruses", one of the most evil periods in history. Would he get a virus if he opened the letter? He remembered the scary stories of his childhood where viruses arose seemingly from nowhere to wipe out memory. But those stories couldn't be true; they were just made up tales. Weren't they?

His next thought was, "if this is from the 1990's, it may be a collectable." Then he remembered that even if it was a collectible it was missing the highly valuable shrink wrap that all written materials came in back then, so it probably wouldn't be worth much anyway.

After much thought and procrastination, the man decided to throw caution to the windmill and open the letter. So he took the letter and placed it in his non-biological de-sheller. After thirty minutes the letter appeared on the product tray.

Looking over the letter the man concluded that it was from the famous educated rapper, Ed. MC Mahon, known for his hardcore rap about how not knowing about your credit is whack and knowing your credit score is wicked; and his heezy, fogelberg, spoken-word rap about the power of gold being able to be turned into cash.

He then wondered why this educated rapper would write him a letter asking him to buy magazines; and why Mahon felt that the chance to win $10,000,000; a relatively small sum, would incent him to do so.

So the man dictated a letter to his ambulatory she-bot computer. The letter simply said, "No thank you." It took him an hour to word it just right.

Using one of the stamps that came with the letter, the man used his Peabody and Sherman Way Back Machine to send the letter to Mahon.

Unfortunately for the man the letter was delivered to the wrong address, where the wrongful recipient wrote, "Return to sender" and placed it back in the mail.

The next day the man, who had not been expecting a letter, received the letter again. Commanding his ambulatory she-bot computer to shake its fist, the man said, "Darn you MC Mahon, you're a crafty son of a photon torpedo; I guess I'll just have to buy some of your magazines or I'll risk getting the Bill Murray disease and be turned into a ground hog."

*****

EXERCISE WS7

Read the business memo that follows and then answer the questions in the next exercise box.

Memo To: All Staff

From: Randall F. Crowl, President

RE: Recent Problems in our Customer Service Dept

Date: November 15, 2012

==

As you are all aware, we have been getting a lot of complaints from our customers regarding our telephone service. To determine if these complaints were the exception or the rule, we sent out surveys to all customers that used our Phone Center in the last three months. The response from our customers was overwhelming. Our response rate from the surveys was 35%, well above industry averages of 20%.

While our response rate for the surveys was good, the results showed that we need a lot of improvement in how our Phone Center performs its customer service functions. The survey results clearly showed that the complaints we were getting from our customers were the rule, not the exception.

Some of the more alarming complaints from our customers were:

- Our phone representatives are sometimes rude to our customers.

- Our phone representatives often lack the knowledge to solve our customers' problems.

- Our customers often wait a long time before their calls are answered or get busy signals.

- When our customers do get through to a phone representative, they are often placed on hold for long intervals.

This is unacceptable! We are implementing a comprehensive plan to correct our poor service. However, to make the plan work we will need the commitment and understanding of our entire staff, especially our phone representatives.

The company will make a significant capital investment in both equipment and staff to correct the problems. But we will also expect more from our phone representatives.

To correct our capacity problem (long wait times before calls are answered and customers getting busy signals) we are purchasing a new phone system that will allow us to have more phone lines. We also plan to hire 10 additional phone representatives. We are making this investment to help both our customers and to ease the work burden on our staff. However, we are also asking for a commitment from our phone representatives. We are implementing a strict policy for time logged into our new phone system. Tardiness will no longer be accepted. If you are supposed to be at your work station and logged into the phone system at 8:00 AM, you must be there at precisely 8:00 AM. 8:01 AM or 8:02 AM will not do!

In addition, we will track every phone representative's talk time. Your goal should be an average talk time of two minutes. Remember, if you spend ten minutes with a customer you are giving that customer great service, but if three other customers have to wait ten minutes before they speak to a phone representative because of that call, we are providing poor service to those three customers. Great service for one and poor service for three is unacceptable. Therefore, manage your talk time.

To correct the other issues that are directly related to the performance of our phone representatives, we plan to implement a comprehensive training program. The training program will cover topics like correct hold procedures, how to remain courteous even when dealing with angry or rude customers, and problem resolution knowledge. The training will be held during your off hours, when you are not scheduled to be on the phone. However, we will pay you double time for attending the training sessions. Once again this is a situation where we are working together to solve our customers' problems. We are making a financial commitment both in terms of paying trainers and paying our phone representatives for additional work hours at twice your normal pay; but we need a commitment from our phone representatives to give up some of their free time and to take our training sessions seriously.

Finally, since we are a business, we need to be sure that our expenditures are worthwhile. Towards that end we will continue to survey our customers, and will start a test call and phone monitoring program.

Last but not least, we are implementing a Phone Representative of the Month award. Each month we will give a $500 check to the Phone Representative of the Month. The Phone Representative of the Month award will go to the phone representative with the highest score on our test call and phone monitoring programs who also has an average talk time of two minutes or less, and has not been late logging into the phone system all month.

Let's continue to work together to improve the service we provide to our customers so we can remain the best company in our industry.

Thank you.

Q1. What is the main idea of this business memo?

A. The company is going to start to track phone representatives more closely.
B. The company is implementing new programs to improve phone service.
C. The company is buying a new phone system.
D. $500 will be given to the top phone representative each month.

Q2. If you were a phone representative, would you react positively or negatively to this memo?

Circle one (no wrong answer):   Positively   Negatively

Using specific details from the memo, give two reasons to support your positive or negative reaction.

_____
_____
_____
_____
_____
_____
_____

Answer the following questions, True or False:

Q3.　　The response rate for the company's survey was industry standards.
　　　　TRUE　　FALSE

Q4.　　Phone representatives now had to log into the phone system in a timely manner. If they were scheduled to log in at 8:00 AM, they could log in at 8:01 AM or 8:02 AM but no later.
　　　　TRUE　　FALSE

Q5.　　The company is making a financial commitment to help solve the problem.
　　　　TRUE　　FALSE

Q6.　　The company is hiring 10 new employees who, in addition to helping with normal phone coverage, will be especially helpful covering for phone representatives that are attending training classes.
　　　　TRUE　　FALSE

Q7.　　The only goal for the test calls and phone monitoring is to help decide who wins the Phone Representative of the Month award.
　　　　TRUE　　FALSE

Q8.　　Every month a $500 check will be given to the employee who is selected as employee of the month.
　　　　TRUE　　FALSE

Reading perceptions in-class group discussion worksheet (from page 39)

1. In the next story Jack is a professional basketball player. Without reading the story what do you know about Jack?

Jack plays professional basketball in the Continental Basketball Association (CBA). He could not make the NBA because he was only 5'5". He is an excellent point guard. However, because the CBA doesn't pay well he has to hold down a second job to pay his bills.

2. In the next story Robin is a cheerleader. Without reading the story what do you know about Robin?

Robin goes to college at the University of Miami. As a former basketball player who hurt his knee, being on the cheerleading squad was a way for him to stay close to the game. His role is to be at the bottom of the cheerleader pyramid, holding up the women who do gymnastics from the top of the pyramid. He himself has no gymnastic or dance skills.

3. On his first day on the job, Stu was nervous and shook hands with his boss using his left hand. Did Stu do anything wrong?

While Stu was nervous, he did not do anything wrong. Stu recently sprained his right shoulder so his right arm was in a sling up against his chest. The only hand he had free to shake his boss' outstretched hand with was his left hand.

Preconceptions and making assumptions are a natural part of pleasure reading. Do not do that on the job.

Business Writing

Very early in my career at Citibank, I wrote a memo explaining why I wanted to change the way the customer service center forecasted future months' call volume from a simplistic approach to a more sophisticated statistical approach. When I completed my five page memo I was very proud. I thought it was the one of the best things I had ever written. I followed the approach I learned in school.

About a day later, the Vice President I wrote the memo for returned it to me and said, "I started reading this and have no idea what it's about so I am returning it to you."

I was crushed. About a year later, after getting a better handle on how to write effectively in the workplace I gave it another shot and the same Vice President said yes to my idea and we implemented the forecasting model for incoming phone calls.

In school I learned writing techniques that included: build to a conclusion, paint a picture with your words, have a powerful ending, etc. This was fine for writing fiction or for making a case in an essay on a test. When writing in the workplace, throw all that out.

The basic strategy for writing in the workplace is simple. *Time is money.* So first, descriptive writing (painting a picture in words) is considered wasteful writing. Both for extra time spent writing the document, and for the extra time required by the reader to read the document. If you want to write that there was a messy desk, just write that there was a messy desk. Do not paint a picture by saying, "There were papers, file folders, discarded food wrappers and more placed seemingly at random all over Jay's desk. If I had dime in my hand I would not have been able to place it directly on the surface of the desk. I would have had to place it on top of a pile of papers or trash and hope, when I came back 15 minutes later, that it wouldn't be buried even deeper in more junk, never to be found again."

At work, the write-up would simply be:

"Jay's desk is very messy. I understand now, why he has trouble finding client files."

This shows not only proper workplace writing, but helps demonstrate what I meant in the prior section about "reading between the lines." The last sentence about never finding the dime again is an example where a writer wants his reader to "read between the lines" to come up with the conclusion that finding required work items could be a problem for Jay given the mess on his desk. At work, if there was concern about Jay finding items at his desk, the memo would be written straight forward like the example shown. If the memo only stated, "Jay's desk is very messy"; then the problem is the mess, do not read into that statement that there has been a problem with Jay finding client files.

The second *time is money* rule for writing in the workplace is that the person you are writing the memo to, needs to be able to determine quickly, the importance of your memo so he/she can allocate the proper amount of time to reading it. In my Citibank example, the Vice President was very busy so when he couldn't get a feel for what the memo was about after reading the first paragraph or two, he decided not to invest the time needed to read, digest, and think about the full five page memo. I needed to get across what the memo was about and the importance of what I was writing about immediately.

That is why writing to build to a conclusion, making your case by building to a big finish is not the proper way to write memos or studies or anything in the workplace.

Writing in the workplace can be demonstrated by the diagram that follows.

Purpose of the memo

Support information: most important

Support information: next most important

Support information: least important

The business memo should open with purpose of your memo. For example: "The current method being used to forecast incoming call volume to the Phone Center is inefficient. It results in more staff expense and poorer service being delivered to our customers, than if a more accurate forecasting method, multiple regression analysis, was used."

What would follow next is support to backup the claim that was just made. You would start with the most important support information, and end with the least important support information. You do not start small, and keep building your case to a climactic conclusion. If you do not get the attention of the readers right away and give them cause to continue reading, they will never make it to the end of your memo containing your climactic conclusion.

As you can see, your writing needs to be direct, organized from most important to least important, and use as few words as possible to make your point. In school your writing assignments often came with "using at least 1,000 words explain <whatever the topic of the writing assignment was>." Your goal was often to write descriptively to add words to reach the minimum goal. In work it is just the opposite. If there was a word goal attached to a work assignment, it would be "using XX words or <u>less</u>, describe your <whatever the topic of the work writing assignment was>." Your goal would be to write straight forward, not descriptively, so you could reach your goal of an effective memo using as few words as possible.

This is yet; again, a difference between how writing assignments are positioned in school versus how writing assignments are completed effectively in the workplace.

Right and Wrong for Business Writing

WRONG – Like a school assignment; using more than 1,000 words write .....
RIGHT – Use as few words as possible

WRONG – Paint a picture using your words
RIGHT – No painting pictures, be direct

WRONG – Allow the reader to reach his or her own conclusion

RIGHT – Tell the reader what conclusion they should reach right up front, then back it up

Business Letter Components

1. Date

2. Company name and address (company stationary is acceptable)

3. The date you are writing the letter

4. A salutation (e.g. Dear Sir or Madam)

5. A first paragraph stating the purpose of the letter

6. Support information (from most important to least important)

7. A closing (e.g. sincerely)

8. Your name with space for your signature between the closing and typed name

9. Phone number and/or e-mail address (optional)

Sample Business Letter

The sample business letter is on the next page.

January 10, 2013

Jay Goldberg, CEO
Name of Company
Street Address
City, State, Zip

Name of Person Sending Letter To, Title
Name of Company
Street Address
City, State, Zip

Dear Mr./Ms. Last Name,

Contents of Letter

Sincerely,

Signature

Name Printed
Title
Phone Number (optional)
E-mail address (optional)

cc: (other people sending letter to; if needed)
encl: (if attach anything to letter indicate what it is, if needed)

Business Memo Components

1. To: Person sending memo to

2. From: Your name

3. RE: (or Subject:) A short sentence regarding the topic of the memo

4. Date: The date the memo is being written

At the bottom of the memo use cc: for all other people you are sending the memo to where you want others to know those people received the memo; cc means carbon copy.

Note – it is considered a common courtesy to cc: anyone who is named in a business memo even if there is no reason for that person to receive that memo. This lets everyone know what others are saying about them first hand and stops rumors.

Business Memo Format

The business memo format should be used at all times with all correspondences, even hand written notes.

To: Randall F. Crowl

From: Jay Goldberg

RE: Work Readiness

Date: 01/10/13

===

Content of memo mentions Duncan Kassel.

CC: D. Kassel

Hand Written Notes

Bad hand written note:

> *Bob*
>
> *The problem we*
> *talked about is still*
> *open.*

Why is this note bad?

What if the note falls on the ground; which Bob gets it?
Is it an old note or a current note?
Bob may be working on numerous problems which one is this?
Who sent the note?

Good hand written note:

> *To: Bob Jones*
> *From: Jay Goldtown*
> *RE: Customer problem - Worldwide*
> *INC.*
> *Date: 1/12/06*
>
> *Bob*
>
> *The problem we*
> *talked about is still*
> *open.*

So take an extra few seconds to put the handwritten note into memo format to eliminate all potential problems. Also keep in mind that had written notes must be legible (easily read by the person you are giving the note to), otherwise they are useless.

EXERCISE WS8

Write a hand written note to your instructor informing him or her of the ranking the top three things you have learned so far in this course that will help you in the workplace. Please use the proper format and proper structure for this assignment.

*****

Understanding Basic Math

In school students are often "hand-held" through math. Many teachers will acknowledge that math is difficult. Hogwash, math is based on logic. If all teachers approached math with the attitude that it is easy, then more students wouldn't feel it was okay if they didn't excel in math. But, that's enough of my soapbox.

In school students get dependent on machines for doing their math (calculators, computer programs, etc.). You would think we would have all learned how bad an idea relying on machines is from the *Terminator* movies. But no, we still rely on machines to perform simple math problems. Don't get me wrong, that would be fine if everyone understood numbers, but many people do not.

Let me give you an example. Let's say you are working a cash register and a customer buys five items and one item was for $100. Then, the total after scanning the price tags shows $101.25. Unless you're working for a store that sells a lot of items for less than thirty cents, and doesn't charge sales tax, something may be wrong. Possibly the $100 product was keyed into the system incorrectly either at the cash register (you), or by the person who entered the prices into the computer (a co-worker). When an error like this happens it often results in products being sold below store prices. Since that negatively impacts the store's profits, that could eventually lead to lower pay raises and employees losing their jobs. Therefore, you need to be able to do basic calculations in your head without relying on "machines", so when an error shows up you can catch it, and question it.

In this case, if you estimated the total amount of the sale in your head, you would know that the total price charged the customer appears to be wrong. Your next step would be to look at the customer's receipt before handing it to him/her. It's possible that an item is on sale. It's also possible that there was an error. Another possibility is that the customer switched tags so that the item printed on the receipt does not match the item the customer is holding.

Whatever the situation is, without understanding numbers, you would not have been able to spot the potential error.

If you spot an error, never accuse the customer, or a co-worker, of doing something wrong. Your workplace should have procedures on how to handle situations like this. If you are not sure what to do, call for a supervisor and explain the situation without blaming anyone. Then allow your supervisor to handle it. Be sure to learn the procedure so the next time you can handle it yourself (unless you are informed that supervisors always handle situations like these).

Here's another example. Your supervisor tells you that a product the company sells for $10 dollars is going on sale for 30% off. He/she then hands you new price tags that show the reduced price and asks you to place them on the products. The price tag says $5.

You need to understand math enough to know that 30% off $10 is not $5. That is half (50%) off. You must be able to catch that error and correct it before placing the new price tags on the items.

Your supervisor handed you the wrong tags. More than likely they were for another product. However, with a big sign that says 30% off on top of the display of those items, if you do not catch the error you will be held accountable. If you fight it by saying you were just doing what you were told, you not only will still be held accountable, but would have just told management through your actions that you are not capable of a role in the company that involves anything more than following orders. You'll remain a "private" in that "corporate army."

By the way, just because you get blamed doesn't mean that your supervisor didn't have his/her head handed to him/her as well. So by not catching the error, you also put your supervisor in a bad position, and this is the person who determines your pay raises. This also means "what's bad for my supervisor could be very bad for me." Being taken to task is not a pleasant experience for your supervisor. You could have, in fact should have; caught the error. So your lack of math knowledge turned you from hero (catching the error so your supervisor avoids an unpleasant experience) to resident of your supervisor's doghouse (not catching the error causing your supervisor to endure an unpleasant experience).

Let me give you one more example. The original price for an item was $10. It has already been marked down 50%. Now your supervisor tells you to mark it down another 50%. Would you know what to do? Well logic tells you that the item is not going to given away for free, so you are not going to take 100% (50% +50%) off the price and mark it down to zero. At least I hope not. So the correct way to mark an item down twice is to do it in two steps. First it was $10, so you take 50% off making

65

it $5. Then you take 50% off the new price ($5), making the price after both discounts are applied $2.50.

You need to understand basic math functions: addition, subtraction, multiplication, division without having to rely on a calculator. Don't get me wrong. Use them. However, if you make a mistake because you entered in wrong numbers, you need to be able to recognize you made an error so that you can correct it. You do this by estimating. For example if a customer buys five items with the following prices:

- $5.12
- $2.98
- $1.22
- $3.86
- $2.01

I would know that the total before taxes would be around $15. I would know this because I would have added $5 + $3 + $1 + $4 + $2 = $15.

I did this by rounding each transaction to the nearest whole dollar ($.01 to $0.49 is rounded down, while $0.50 to $0.99 is rounded up).

When the total came out to $15.19, I would have known that everything appeared right.

However, if the total came out to $12.19, because I accidentally entered $3.86 as $0.86, I would have known that the total appeared low and checked the receipt.

Know one thing, errors that favor the business are almost always caught and if not, result in lost customers. However, errors favoring the customers are often not caught resulting in the business losing money. There are ethical people who will mention if there is an error in their favor, but not all people act ethically in that situation (which can result in the employee being fired, or docked pay, but they do not think about that).

There are some businesses that honor incorrect prices that favor customers when products are tagged incorrectly by one of their employees. The business will honor that sale and then immediately correct the price tags on the remainder of products. But, how happy do you think management is that the business sold a product at a lower than expected price because of a mistake by an employee? If that happened because an employee relied on a calculator and had no idea the result was wrong because he/she doesn't understand numbers, how well do you think that excuse will fly? Well, I'll tell you; not very far.

Here is another example. You work on a machine in a manufacturing plant. The machine is supposed to produce 100 products an hour. The machine starts at 7:00 AM every day. You work the second shift and get in at noon. You look over and see only 250 items completed so far that day. Using your math skills, you know that there should have been 500 items (5 *100; 5 hours with 100 items produced per hour). So you inform your supervisor that something is wrong. Since you caught the problem early and production is only 2.5 hours behind it can be made up that day and the customer order can still be filled on time. If it wasn't spotted until it was time to pack the order (let's say two days later), the customer order would have been delayed resulting in the customer receiving the order late. If receiving orders on a timely basis was crucial to that customer, that customer could decide to no longer do business with your company. That would mean fewer profits and that could mean fewer jobs or reduced hours, or lower wages. So if you caught the production problem early, your basic math skills would have saved the company from a potentially harmful result.

Quick Multiplication

There are some tricks you can use to multiply without using a calculator. Break the problem down into its component parts and then add those pieces together. Some examples follow:

Problem: 33 x 99

Step one: multiply 33 x 100 = 3300
Step two: subtract 33 (problem was 99, not 100) = 3300 - 33 = 3267

Problem: 56 x 12
Step one: multiply 56 x 10 = 560
Add two more 56's to that total = 560 + 112 = 672

Problem 15 x 220

Step one: multiply 220 x 10 = 2200
Step two: take half of the result above (5 x 220 is half of 10 x220)
half of 2200 = 1100
Step three: add the parts together = 2200 + 1100 = 3300

Problem 124 x 80

Step one: multiply 124 x 100 = 12,400
Step two: multiply 124 x 20 = 2,480
Step three: subtract 2,500 (to use an easier number) from 12,400
= 12,400 – 2,500 = 9,900
Step four: add 20 back in (subtracted 2,500 instead of 2,480) = 9,900 -20 = 9,920

Fractions and Percents

To change a fraction to a percent, divide the numerator by the denominator.

To change a decimal to a percent, multiply it by 100

1/2 (numerator/denominator)

1 dived by 2 = .5

.5 x 100 = 50%

3/8 (numerator/denominator)

3 divide by 8 = .375

.375 x 100 = 37.5%

5/2 (numerator/denominator)

5 divided by 2 = 2.5

2.5 x 100 = 250%

Percent change

Comparing old to new:

1. Subtract the old value from the new value.
2. Divide the difference by the old value

So if you earned $40,000 last year (old value) and earned $50,000 this year (new value):

$50,000 - $40,000 = $10,000
$10,000/$40,000 = 25%

So you earned 25% more this year as compared to last year.

Comparing new to old:

1. Subtract the new value from the old value
2. Divide by the new value

So in the prior case:

$40,000 - $50,000 = -$10,000
-$10,000/$50,000 = -20%

So you earned 20% less last year than you earned this year.

Therefore, when doing percent changes, it is important what you are using as the base for comparison (e.g. current as compared to past – first example; or past as compared to current, second example).

EXERCISE WS9

1.   In 2011 a baseball player had a batting average of 290, had 30 home runs and 100 RBI. In 2012 that same player improved to a batting average of 300, hit 40 home runs and knocked in 120 RBI. What was the baseball player's percent improvement in 2012, over 2011 in each of these three categories? (HINT – 2011 is the base)

2.   A business owner earned $80,000 in profits in 2011. Revenues (sales) were $200,000 and costs were $120,000.

If costs are expected to be $130,000 in 2012, and revenues are expected to be $225,000, what is the percent increase in profits expected to be in 2012? (HINT, Profits = Revenues – Expenses). What is growing at a faster rate, revenues or expenses? (HINT – you must calculate profits for 2012 before you can answer the questions)

3.   The regular price for books is $2.50. However, there is a 20% discount if you buy 100 or more. What is the discount price for buying 100 or more books? What is the total product cost if you buy 200 books? What is the total product cost if you buy 10 books?

4.   The regular price for desks is $100. However, there is a 10% discount if you buy 10 or more. What is the total product cost if you buy 60 desks? If the customer is given an additional 10% off at the register, what will the price now be for the 60 books?

5.   Your original price for music CDs is $14. What is the sale price if you mark it down 10%?

6.   Your original price for computers is $1,000. What is the sale price if you mark it down 30%?

7.   Your cost for puppies is $100. What is your selling price if you want to make 75% on each puppy?

8.   The original price for a book is $30. It has been discounted 10% already. Your supervisor asks you to mark it down an additional 10%. Does that make the sale price $24 or $24.30?

9.   True or false. As long as I have a calculator, computer and point of sale terminal, it is okay if I do not

understand numbers; these devices will always give me the correct results.

10.   True or false. Math is very difficult for many people so I know all my supervisors will understand and not hold me accountable if I do not catch simple math errors at work.

*****

Advanced Workplace Skills

In video games there are special codes that allow you to advance faster, or have more fun by using items, or have powers not available without those special codes. Well, in work, there are skills you can develop that do the same thing. By mastering these skills you will see your compensation grow faster because you will be more valuable in the workplace, and you'll advance to jobs that will be more fun and rewarding since the jobs will make more use of your advance skills.

The "special codes" (advanced workplace skills) that follow will help you become very valuable in the workplace.

Problem-solving skills

Steps you can take to help you come up with solutions for solving problems follow:

> 1. Understand the problem – this means more than just understanding the obvious. Write down the impact the problem has on everyone affected by the problem.

> 2. Determine the cause of the problem – knowing the cause of the problem helps ensure that the solutions fix the root cause.

3. Identify the current solution – the current solution is not working; know what it is and why it is not working so your new solution is not just a re-hashing of the old, ineffective solution.

4. Come up with possible solutions – here is where you can be creative; first write down anything that comes to mind, even if it does not initially make sense, or you cannot see how to implement it. For example, if the problem is that not enough people know about the store you work for, you could write down, "go to the busy corner of fifth and main, get a bullhorn, and talk about your store." Just be sure that the possible solutions solve the problem and are not re-treads of the existing solution that is not working.

5. Identify real-life solutions for the possible solutions – look at your list of possible solutions and try to think of a way to implement them. You may not be able to do this with all of your possible solutions. For the example in step 4, a real-life solution could be to place a billboard at the busy corner of 5th and main, or a sign on the bus that picks people up at the 5th and Main bus stop, as well as other heavily trafficked spots.

6. Rank the solutions – after coming up with possible real-life solutions, rank them. If a real-life solution does not make much sense at this point, eliminate it from your list.

7. Present the solutions to your supervisor – inform your supervisor, either in writing or verbally, of the solutions you've come up with for the problem. Present them in order from best to worst. Allow your supervisor to pick

the one he/she likes best, even if it is not on the top of your list. Your supervisor will have other criteria (such as cost, time frames, prior experience, etc.) which could change your order.

8. Follow through – if your supervisor uses you to implement the solution to the problem (e.g., come up with the wording for the billboard), be sure to complete that assignment fully in a timely manner.

9. Monitor the results – an area where some employees and even supervisors fall short is that they do not track the results of what they implement to fix a problem. For example, if a billboard is placed at 5th and main so that more people know about the store you work for, there needs to be a way to determine if the billboard is doing its job. You cannot assume because more people come to the store that it was because of the billboard. It may be a sale that is going on in the store, or that a new business opened across the street so you are getting some of their overflow customers. So there needs to be a way to monitor the effectiveness of the solution. If you can think of one, discuss it with your supervisor and implement it, and you will be a very valuable employee indeed. In this case, asking a couple of questions of customers in the store and tracking the results will go a long way towards knowing the effectiveness of the billboard. For example you can ask the customer, "How did you find out about our store?"

Problem-solving worksheet

Sales in the restaurant you work for, a diner, has declined by 30% over the last three months. It is also down 30% over the same three month period last year. The drop off is not due to the economy. Other restaurants in the area have not seen a reduction in sales. In addition, a new diner which opened six months ago appears to be growing its business significantly.

1. What is the problem?

_____

_____

_____

_____

_____

2. What are some possible consequences of this problem?

_____

_____

_____

_____

_____

3. What are some possible causes for this problem?

_____

_____

_____

_____

_____

4. What are some steps you could take to try to determine the real cause(s) of this problem?

_____

_____

_____

_____

_____

5. Choose one of the causes you listed in question 3 and indicate three solutions you could take to help solve the problem.

_____

_____

_____

_____

_____

6. Rank your three solutions in order from most likely to fix the problem to least likely to fix the problem.

   1. _____

       _____

       _____

   2. _____

       _____

       _____

   3. _____

       _____

       _____

7. How would you track whether or not your top solution (#1 above) was working (note – not just that sales increased but that your solution is the reason sales have increased)

_____

_____

_____

_____

Creative thinking

Creative thinking is often called thinking outside the box. Mastering this skill is a sure fire way to make yourself valuable in the workplace. Why? Unlike other workplace skills, which get the same results from every worker, the results from the creative thinking process varies by worker.

Creative thinking is a way for you to stand out in the workplace. If management values your creative thought process in solving problems, management knows if you leave, the person who replaces you will not come up with the same creative solutions that you did.

Creative thinking comes natural to some, and must be honed and developed by others. If you are someone who could see himself/herself writing a good detective story one day, you probably have good creative thinking skills. If you read or watch a good "who did it" book or movie and marvel at how the writer put together the clues to solve the fictional case, you may have to work on these skills.

As an example, let's use one of my favorite movies, *Armageddon*. In the movie a giant asteroid is hurtling towards earth and if it hits, it will destroy all life on the planet. After looking at, and dismissing, all of the obvious solutions, they decide to send astronauts to drill in the asteroid to a depth where a nuclear bomb will split the asteroid and the two main pieces will the bypass earth.

Knowing that drilling is too tough to learn in the time they have, the Bruce Willis character recommends that they send his teams of deep-core drillers to the asteroid to do the work.

That combination of drilling on the asteroid and using non-astronauts to go into space is an example of thinking outside the box, hence a creative solution.

A Strategy for Continuing Education

When it comes to taking continuing/community education courses many people react in the moment; they look at the course offerings at the local venue, and decide to take a course that will be fun or helpful.

For career purposes, the better way to approach continuing education is determine what subjects will help you grow in your career, and look for courses in a variety of venues that offer the courses you want.

This is subtle difference, but a big one. The first is going with the flow, the second is goal oriented.

For example, you may need Excel and Access knowledge to be eligible for a promotion, but only see a course for Excel at the local venue and take that course. Then you sit back and wait for a course in Access in that venue. That course may not be offered there for a year and a half, if at all. Here it was good that you got knowledge in Excel, but your goal should have been both Excel and Access to put yourself in a position to get promoted.

This also means that you need to look at the higher level positions in the company and determine the skills needed to put yourself in a position to advance in the company. Remember, it is not what you think will be helpful, it is what management thinks will be helpful.

One strategy is to ask someone in management or in human resources what they recommend you learn to help you advance in the company. It is best to do this after you have had enough time in the company to demonstrate that you have strong work readiness skills. If you do this at that time, management could keep an eye on you since they know you are a very good employee who is looking to stay with and advance in the company.

On the other hand, if you do this too early, before demonstrating your value as an employee, management may feel you are being too aggressive, or that you are not satisfied performing the job you were hired to do. Also, if you have time on the job and have not performed your work readiness skills well, management may feel that you should concentrate on performing better in the workplace before you worry about getting a promotion.

Next, understand that businesses market their product and services to get customers. Most do not sit back and wait for customers, on their own, to find out what the business sells.

This means that you must let your supervisor (and human resources) know that you are taking a course in a subject matter that will help the business. Don't oversell, but be direct and let the people in charge of promotions know you are taking steps to put yourself in a position to get a promotion.

Continuing education worksheet

List three areas (specific topics or courses or programs) you would like to pursue through continuing education (either formally though a degree or certification program or informally through a community education course) to help you grow in your job or in your career.

1. _____

    How will this area help your career?

    _____

2. _____

How will this area help your career?

_____

3. _____

How will this area help your career?

_____

Report Generation and Analysis

This advanced skill uses the other skills written about previously in this book. For example, you know you have to write your report using the business writing approach; that you need to spell everything out since the readers will not be reading between the lines; that your math skills will come in handy during the analysis; that new skills you obtained through continuing education could also help you throughout the process; and that following the problem-solving steps and using your creative thinking skills will help you come up with solutions to any problems uncovered by your report.

This is all while managing you time effectively, being sure to not just undertake the task, but complete the report, following any company or department directions for writing and distributing your report, and updating associated procedure manuals if changes are made to any procedure or policy based on the recommendations in your report.

Charts and Graphs

Charts are an easy way to display a lot of detailed information in a report. Be sure to have column headings that clearly indicate the information being reported in that column. If you use any abbreviations in the column headings, use an asterisk (*) and at the bottom of the chart indicate the full title.

Here is a sample chart:

Jay's Fantasy Football Roster Breakdown

*Position	How many	Percent of Roster
QB	2	16.7%
RB	3	20.0%
WR	3	20.0%
TE	2	16.7%
K	1	8.3%
DEF	1	8.3%

*QB = quarterback, RB = running back, WR = wide receiver, TE = tight end, K = kicker, DEF = team defense

In addition to charts, graphs are another way to effectively show detailed information. Using a spreadsheet program such as Excel can turn charts into graphs. A graph that could have been used in the previous exercise is:

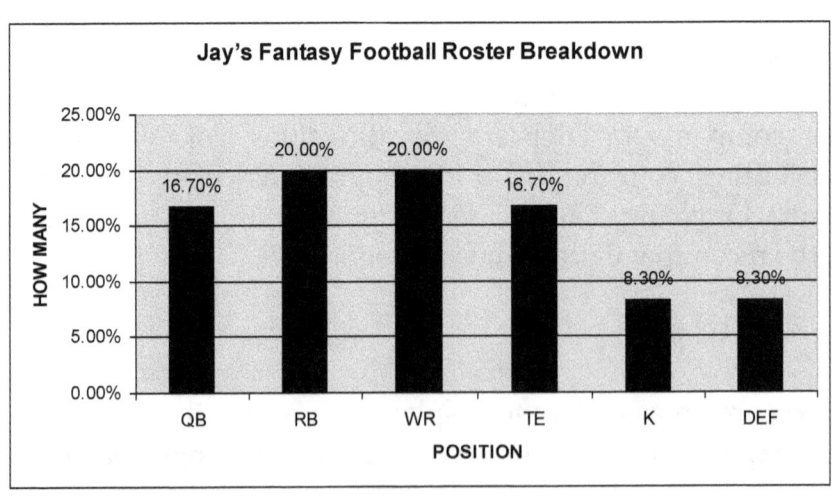

As you can see the graph contains the same information as the chart, the number players by position.

EXERCISE WS10

You are assigned to determine how effectively your supervisor's secretary is answering the phone. This includes the time it takes for the calls to be answered, as well as what the secretary says while on the phone. Your supervisor states that the goal is to have all the calls answered with no more than four rings and for the secretary to never make the company look bad to the person calling.

So your supervisor sets you up to monitor (listen in) on all of the secretary's calls for one day. You ask your supervisor if the secretary knows you will be monitoring and he/she says, yes, and wants the secretary informed as to what you find.

There are ten calls. This is what you find:

Call #	# Rings Before Answered	Comments	Professional & Courteous
1	3	Nothing negative	Yes
2	2	Nothing negative	Yes
3	5	Nothing negative	Yes
4	4	Nothing negative	Yes
5	2	Said supervisor not back from lunch yet	Yes
6	3	Nothing negative	Yes
7	1	Nothing negative	Yes
8	4	Said supervisor too busy to take any calls now	Yes
9	2	Nothing negative	Yes
10	3	Nothing negative	Yes

Use the business memo format and business writing techniques and etiquette to write a report to your supervisor (use the name of your instructor as your supervisor's name). The secretary's name is Pat Jones. Also include a chart summarizing the 10 calls by number of rings.

*****

EXERCISE WS11

Q1. Use the information below to fill in the form that follows. (The plant is open 24 hours a day, be sure that the information for time is entered precisely)

Jack Smith is finished cleaning machine ABC at 8:50 AM, and machine JAY at 10:15 AM. Jack also sets machine ABC at 8:55 AM and machine JAY at 10:20 AM.

Mary Jones completes the test for machine XYZ at 7:00 AM and machine ABC at 9:30 AM.

Lisa LaDonna verifies that the model 15 blades are the right size at 2:15 PM, she counts 100 blades. She then verifies that the model 25 blades are the right size at 3:30 PM, she counts 200 blades.

Cassie Douglas finishes assembling the model 15 blades at 5:30 PM. There are 100 of them.

Arthur Batman starts his quality control of the model 15 blades at 8:30 PM, and passes 95.

Q2. How many model 15 blades did not pass the quality control inspection?

Harold's Collectible Knives, Inc. Task Checklist

Enter first name and last initial upon successful completion of each task

Date:_____

FABRICATION Blanking the blades	Name	Time
Machine XYZ cleaned		
Machine XYZ set		
Machine XYZ tested		
Machine ABC cleaned		
Machine ABC set		
Machine ABC tested		
Machine JAY cleaned		
Machine JAY set		
Machine JAY tested		

COMPLETION Knife assembly	Name	Quantity
Model 15 blade proper size		
Model 15 blade spinning		
Model 15 blade bracketing		
Model 15 final assembly		
Model 25 blade proper size		
Model 25 blade spinning		
Model 25 blade bracketing		
Model 25 final assembly		
# passed quality control		
model 15		m15 ____
model 25		m25 ____

Certification Scenarios

Workplace Skills Scenario 1

Olivia walks past the desk of her co-worker, Charlie, and can see by the look on his face that he is very upset. She asks him, "What's wrong?" Charlie tells Olivia that he gave what he thought was an excellent ten page report to their supervisor, Broyles, and he looked at it briefly, and handed it back to him saying I don't have the time to read this." Olivia then asks Charlie if she can read the report. Charlie responded, "That would be great!"

The report started as follows:

"There are major problems in the workplace. Before stating what they are, let me inform you how this situation came about.

It all started five years ago before you were put in charge of this department. Back then ...."

The report then goes through the history spending about seven pages on the past before stating the problems. Furthermore, Olivia notices, there are generalizations, not specifics in the report as it relates to the problem, and the report contains no possible solutions to the problem. However, the report did highlight some real problems that definitely needed to be addressed.

So Olivia asks Charlie if it would be okay if they worked together to write a memo to Broyles, to alert him about the problems and that they include some suggestions to fix the problems in the memo. Charlie answers, "Why not; we need to try to get Broyles to see what is happening."

Before writing the memo, Olivia and Charlie needed to come up with some possible solutions to the problems.

Olivia says, "Why don't we start now; there is no time like the present." Charlie agrees.

Unbeknownst to Olivia is that Charlie has to get a package out to a customer, Nina, by 2:00 PM so that it could be guaranteed for delivery the next day. Since it was 1:00 PM, and the packaging task would only take Charlie 30 minutes, he feels he can push that task back a bit to attack the solutions to the problems since solving the problems is very important, and working on the solutions is a lot more fun and meaningful than the manual labor associated with the packaging task. In fact, Charlie thinks, packaging the product isn't my normal work anyway, I was only doing it because Lincoln is on vacation.

As they begin to brainstorm ideas, Charlie immediately starts throwing out possible solutions. Some make sense, some do not. Some of his solutions rely on processes that Olivia believes are breaking down and causing the problem. However, Charlie is on a roll and Olivia cannot get a word in edgewise to slow him down. Finally Charlie does slows down, and says " I need to take a break" and heads to the vending machine on the fourth floor.

When Charlie comes back from break he looks at his watch and sees that the time is 1:50 PM. He immediately tells Olivia he has something he needs to do and they should meet up again in 30 minutes.

During the time Charlie is away, Olivia does some work to provide a solid background so that the solutions they both come up with will make more sense.

Charlie comes back 30 minutes later right after he finishes packaging the product for delivery to Nina. They continue the work on the memo and it goes very well. In fact they talk to Peter and Walter, who run the phone monitoring program, to get more detailed information to help dimension the problem. Below is the memo that Olivia and Charlie write:

Memo To: Broyles Phillips

From: Olivia Completed-Ham
             Charlie Multiple-Franks

RE: Issues in our Customer Service
             Department

Date: November 15, 2012

==

During our routine monitoring of customer calls, we noticed some complaints from our customers regarding our telephone service.

Some of the more alarming complaints from our customers were:

- our phone representatives are sometimes rude to our customers
- our phone representatives often lack the knowledge to solve our customer's problems
- our customers often wait a long time on hold before talking to a customer service representative
- when our customers do get through to a phone representative, they are often placed on hold for long intervals

In addition the number of complaints we have noticed has increased this month over last month.

In both months we monitored 80 calls. The table that follows summarizes our findings:

Complaint	Last Month	This Month
Rude	3	11
Lack of Knowledge	4	3
Long Wait Time	10	14
On Hold Too Long	3	5
TOTAL PROBLEMS	20	30

Since we get over 10,000 calls a month, the 80 monitored calls is not a significant number of samples.

<NOTE - Olivia recently took a course in statistics and it included sample size analysis; and took a course in market research that included the correct way to construct, field and analyze a survey; Broyles, her supervisor, does not know this>

Therefore, we believe that the first step is to field a survey to help dimension the problem.

We further recommend that the survey be conducted monthly so that we can track the problems over time. This helps in two ways:

- first, if there is no major problem, to ensure it is staying that way
- second, if there is a major problem, to determine if the solutions implemented are fixing the problem

In either case, the phone monitoring is highlighting specific incidences where problems are occurring. So our second recommendation is that we set up refresher training courses which phone representatives who show a pattern of errors during monitoring, are required to attend.

Our third recommendation is to update our procedure manual. It is out of date regarding some of the problem resolutions so the phone representatives do not use it. If it was updated, the phone representatives could use it if they find themselves in a situation where they lack the knowledge to resolve a customer problem.

As an aside, many phone representatives look at the monitoring in a very negative light. In addition to using it as a tool to spot errors, you could give some thought to rewarding phone representatives who continually perform perfectly on the monitored calls.

We want to thank Peter and Walter Rook for providing us with the numbers that are contained in this memo.

cc: P. Rook
    W. Rook

After reading the memo, Broyles assigns Peter Rook the task of fielding the survey. Peter has experience with monitoring calls, but has no experience generating and fielding surveys. Remembering that Charlie was the original person to approach him about this problem, he assigns Charlie the task of making a proposal regarding rewarding employees who continually perform well on monitored calls.

Charlie discusses some initial ideas with Broyles in regards to a reward program for employees who continually perform well on monitored calls. Broyles is very impressed and believes Charlie may be on to something good. However, one week, two weeks, one month later, Broyles doesn't get a report from Charlie. Two months later, still no report from Charlie, and Broyles gets wrapped up in a new problem and all thoughts of a program rewarding employees who continually perform well on monitored calls is completely off his mind.

Workplace Skills Scenario 2

Daryl and Merle are brothers who work at the fast food restaurant Hershel's Fresh Farm Burgers. The burgers are so tasty, that the company's slogan, "Our burgers are so good zombies prefer them to all alternatives," rings true.

Hershel's Fresh Farm Burgers has a company policy, clearly stated in the employee handbook, that all leftover food is thrown out at the end of the day; and that no employee can take any of the food leftover at the end of the day home, for any reason.

At the end of the night, their supervisor, Maggie, leaves the restaurant allowing the brothers to close up shop. Immediately upon Maggie's leaving Merle notices his brother Daryl take four leftover Hershel Fresh Farm burgers and place them aside to take home. The only other person in the restaurant at that time, a local customer named Glenn, also notices Daryl putting the leftover burgers aside to take home. Glenn also witnesses Merle observing Daryl putting the burgers in a bag to take home.

Merle knows what Daryl is doing is against company policy, but he thinks the policy is dumb. Why waste food? Besides, it's not like Maggie can call the sheriff, Rick, and have Daryl arrested. In fact, Merle knows that Daryl is doing a good thing for a struggling family. Daryl has always had a crush on Carol; Carol's daughter Sophia loves Hershel's burgers; and Carol is struggling to make ends meet since the untimely death of her husband Ed. Merle thinks it all adds up, it's good for everyone involved; and it hurts no one.

So Darryl leaves with the burgers, and Merle follows him out the door minutes later. There he notices Glenn writing notes on some forms. What was that all about thinks Merle?

The Author's Training Philosophy

When I was hired to develop a work readiness curriculum in 2002 there were already a number of established work readiness training programs. With employers complaining about the lack of job skills and poor workplace behaviors by their employees in focus groups throughout the United States, I knew I had to develop more than a training curriculum; I needed to create a better way to deliver workplace training.

First, let's look at traditional programs.

Traditional Programs

Practically all workplace training programs follow models used in education. That means that they are assessment based. FCAT, SAT, etc., determine success in education and, similarly, a certification test determines success in many workplace training courses. And once workplace training ends there is no formal process to hold the individuals trained accountable for what they learned during training.

In fact, assessment tests have become so important in education that schools not only teach students knowledge, but teach students how to take tests. They must. After all, funding is often tied to their students' performances on tests such as the FCAT. Certainly many high school juniors and seniors enroll in courses to help them learn how to improve their SAT scores. And this is not just the case with kids. How many construction management schools, real estate schools, and even schools to help with the BAR exam for attorneys are out there? These schools often teach their students how to take and pass tests.

What does this mean? It means that if a student truly knows only 55% of the required knowledge, but can reduce the other questions to a possible 1 in 3 choice, the laws of probability conclude that the student's expected result on the test is 70%.

Even worse, if a student truly knows only 60% of the required knowledge, but can reduce the other questions to a possible 1 in 2 choice, the laws of probability conclude that the student's expected result on the test is 80%. That means a student whose knowledge base is an "F" (60% was failing grade when I went to school), appears to be a "B" student.

While educators cling to the argument that assessment tests are good indicators of success, no one can make that case when dealing with job skills and behaviors. As an example let's use the following multiple choice question:

If you wake up in the morning and your car will not start, you should:

A) Have made prior arrangements with a coworker who lives in your neighborhood to serve as an emergency ride to work.

Whether because of actual knowledge or eliminating answers like, "B) Take as many days off of work as you need to get your car fixed," someone answering this question correctly does not mean that that is the behavior he or she will follow if this situation actually happened to him or her. Workplace training is NOT about answering questions correctly. It's about doing the right thing in the workplace. That is accomplished through training materials that not only teach what is expected in the workplace, but *why* that skill/behavior is important in the workplace; and also uses real life examples that everyone can relate to outside of the workplace to help illustrate key points. In workplace training, it is the journey (curriculum) that is the key, not the final destination (assessment test). This is because success is measured in the attitudes changed and instilled in participants, not on how much work readiness knowledge they possess.

While this may be obvious to you and me, it isn't obvious to the powers that be. For example, instead of investing in a structured program with an effective curriculum that would produce high-quality employees that employers could rely on; many states either independently or in groups decided to spend funds on generating work readiness credentials through assessment testing. They appear to care more about formulating the perfect question, than the perfect learning tool.

Work readiness certification test results from programs that do not have effective curriculum that changes and shapes attitudes, are, at best, an indicator for possible success and, at worst, a false hope for the business community that hires the "credentialed graduates."

Jay Goldberg's Workplace Training Philosophy

I have been developing and fine-tuning my workplace training program and philosophy since 2002. What follows is a list of the key components for what I know is the correct way to implement a workplace training program.

(1) The client for employee training programs is the **business community** first, and the classroom participants second. Why? Employers observing the participants in the workplace will ultimately determine if the training program is successful; not

how well the participants perform in class or on tests. In addition, if employers like the program and believe they can rely on the participants who successfully complete the training to perform well in the workplace; they will value, hire and promote graduates of the program. And that is the main reason the participants are taking the training; to get jobs, keep jobs, and grow in their jobs. In other words, participants want to increase their value to employers.

This realization separates the training programs developed and implemented by the author from most of the other programs in the marketplace. Schools (for sure) and most other venues as well, take on the strategy to improve their students as much as possible, and then market them as vigorously as they can to the marketplace. The result is often graduates, who the school/ training venue expect may fall short of expectations, getting hired and, in fact, falling short of expectations. This result hurts future graduates of the program.

Therefore, my workplace training programs do not allow participants to achieve full certification unless they demonstrate that the main client (the business community) will be able to rely on them at work.

(2) A curriculum that not only teaches what is expected, but why that skill/behavior is important in the workplace, and uses real life examples that everyone can relate to outside of the workplace to illustrate key points, is the foundation to having a successful workplace training program. By clearly defining important workplace skills and behaviors, and informing participants why those skills and behaviors are important to employers; the program sets a baseline of understanding and helps change the participants' attitudes and behaviors.

(3) The training needs to be run like a place of business not a typical educational classroom. The instructor is not just the trainer, but during training is the supervisor, and the participants treat each other as co-workers, not training buddies or friends.

(4) After taking workplace training courses, exams (certification exams or otherwise) are used NOT to indicate competency, but to demonstrate that the participants understood the concepts taught during training so that their employers can start holding them accountable for demonstrating those competencies on the job.

(5) Since performance on the job is what is important to employers, the key program assessments are not the exams, but demonstrated competencies the participants prove every day in class. This also helps the participants understand how they will be evaluated on the job. As an example, during training, a participant demonstrates the ability to not be tardy by never being late to a training session and never extending breaks during a training session.

(6) Since certified program graduates will have shown that they understand the concepts taught during training, and that they can follow some simple, basic rules that are employed during training (through demonstrated competencies); employers should be encouraged to incorporate the competency statements in the training program into their employees' formal performance appraisals.

(7) Within the training program, all competency statements must be very well defined. There should be no leeway given to individual trainers in scoring pass/fail on competencies.

(8) Hold the participants accountable for meeting <u>all</u> their competencies. Recommend to the employers you work with to help place your graduates, that they tie individual compensation (raises, bonuses, etc.) and individual/work unit rewards (employee of the month, monthly pizza party, etc.) to their employees' performances in meeting their competencies.

(9) In addition to training participants, if there are multiple people giving the training sessions, there needs to be a consistent approach between all trainers. That means there may need to be train-the-trainer sessions to ensure all trainers conduct their training in a consistent manner. This is especially true given that the participants will be held accountable for implementing what they learn in the training session every day on the job. Knowing that everyone was trained the same way provides role models who completed the program, were hired, and are now succeeding in the workplace. And since these former program participants received the exact same training as the current participants, there are no excuses for the current participants to fail once they enter the workplace. Program consistency between trainers means no former graduate will be ale to use the excuse, "my instructor never taught me that" to their employer who hired them because of their work readiness credential.

(10) As you can see my program philosophy is very intricate and everything must work in concert to ensure optimal success. Therefore, in addition to instructor training there must be instructor audits to ensure that all teachers/trainers are following and teaching the program correctly.

Jay Goldberg's Background in Work Readiness

As mentioned previously, in 2002 I was hired to develop a work readiness curriculum that I grew into a work readiness

100

philosophy and program. The program I developed was called the best work readiness certification program in the United States by a member of the National Skills Standard Board at a presentation of the Program in Jacksonville, Florida on 01/13/03.

The results from my initial client far exceeded those of other work readiness programs. Employers lined up to hire the graduates and found that over 85% of the graduates remained employed six months later, and over 30% received promotions.

Later I modified and added to the program for a second client.

Since that time I wrote a well-reviewed work readiness book for individuals titled, *How to Get, Keep and Be Well Paid in a Job* (Outskirts Press, ISBN: 9781432725297).

Now I have constructed a four module work readiness and customer service training program that can be used in teaching venues and for on the job training. The four modules each come with recommended competencies and a final online certification test (to use as proof of knowledge so that these individuals can now be held accountable for demonstrating what they leaned every day at work). Participants should have to pass all of the competencies in order to be eligible to sit for the certification test.

About the Author

Jay Goldberg, MBA, is a former Service Director for Citibank. At Citibank, Mr. Goldberg specialized in customer service management, measurement, training, capacity planning, profitability, MIS reporting, and strategic planning.

After almost fourteen years with Citibank, Mr. Goldberg left to form his own consulting firm, DTR Inc. DTR Inc. specializes in writing business plans, developing workplace training programs, designing and implementing customer service strategies, performing strategic planning and market research (e.g., surveys, focus groups, etc.), helping businesses build their brands, and training managers and employees.

At DTR Inc., Mr. Goldberg developed the program parameters, program strategy, curriculum, lesson plans, assessments, competency statements, and certification tests for a Work Readiness Training Program called the best Work Readiness Certification Program in the United States by a representative of the National Skills Standard Board at a presentation of the Program in Jacksonville, Florida on 01/13/03.

Mr. Goldberg later updated, modified and added to that Program for a second client and wrote a book, "How to Get, Keep and Be Well Paid in a Job" (ISBN = 9781432725297), specifically tailored to individuals looking to improve their work readiness skills.

In 2007, Mr. Goldberg was instrumental in helping the Palm Beach County Resource Center develop a revolutionary Entrepreneurship Training Program. The program's structure was unlike any other in the marketplace, and would prove to be highly successful.

In 2012, Mr. Goldberg's entrepreneurship book, "Building a Successful Business," (ISBN = 9781470000639) was published. The book is now being used as a textbook for entrepreneurship courses. The book is both a textbook and a workbook with tools entrepreneurs can use to help start, grow and manage their businesses.

While at the Palm Beach County Resource Center, Mr. Goldberg worked with hundreds of small businesses and got a good handle on how to best structure and implement a work readiness training program to ensure that the benefits of training would be demonstrated in the workplace.

In 2013 Mr. Goldberg published his book for his comprehensive work readiness and customer service training program. There is a teacher book, a classroom book (without answers) and PowerPoint presentations available in the full program.

Contact Mr. Goldberg at Book@DTRConsulting.BIZ. Be sure to write "your work readiness book" in the subject line to ensure that your email is not deleted as junk mail. His business's web site is www.DTRConsulting.BIZ.

Rock Trees: The Beatles: Volume 1: The Paul McCartney Tree
By JAY GOLDBERG

ISBN = 9781494739102

Six Degrees of Separation was originally proposed by Frigyes Karinthy. The theory says that everyone in the world can be connected through a maximum of six steps. Applying that theory to The Beatles, this book shows how 1,550 bands/artists connect back to The Beatles.

This is Volume One of a planned series and examines the Paul McCartney "Rock Tree." The other Beatles will get their own books in the future.

The book contains fifty "rock trees" each with thirty one bands/artists per tree and each with a companion chart showing how the bands are connected.

The goal was not to repeat any band/artist, although musicians can be solo artists and parts of different bands. I accomplished that goal.

Only band members or guest or studio musicians or singers were used to connect the bands/artists. Song writing, production, engineering, etc. credits did not count.

FOR MORE INFORMATION VISIT
www.createspace.com/4580254